MONERANS & PROTISTS

MONERANS & PROTISTS

DR. ALVIN, VIRGINIA, AND ROBERT SILVERSTEIN

TWENTY-FIRST CENTURY BOOKS

A Division of Henry Holt and Company
New York

Twenty-First Century Books
A Division of Henry Holt and Company, Inc.
115 West 18th Street
New York, NY 10011

Henry Holt® and colophon are trademarks of
Henry Holt and Company, Inc.
Publishers since 1866

Published in Canada by Fitzhenry & Whiteside Ltd.
195 Allstate Parkway, Markham, Ontario L3R 4T8

Library of Congress Cataloging-in-Publication Data
Silverstein, Alvin.
Monerans and protists / Alvin Silverstein, Virginia Silverstein, and Robert Silverstein. — 1st ed.
p. cm. — (The Kingdoms of life)
Includes index.
Summary: Describes these single–celled organisms and explains their importance in maintaining the ecosystem.
1. Microbiology—Juvenile literature. 2. Prokaryotes—Juvenile literature. 3. Protista—Juvenile literature. [1. Microbiology.]
I. Silverstein, Virginia B. II. Silverstein, Robert A. III. Title. IV. Series: Silverstein, Alvin. The Kingdoms of life.
QR57.S54 1996   95–42322
576—dc20   CIP
                                                                        AC

ISBN 0-8050-3521-4
First Edition 1996

Designed by Kelly Soong

Printed in the United States of America
All first editions are printed on acid-free paper ∞.
10 9 8 7 6 5 4 3 2 1

Photo credits

Cover: Sinclair Stammers/SPL/Photo Researchers, Inc.

p. 6 (clockwise from top right): Dave B. Fleetham/Tom Stack & Associates; Rod Planck/Tom Stack & Associates; Cabisco/Visuals Unlimited; M. I. Walker/Photo Researchers, Inc.; Zig Leszczynski/Earth Scenes; Bill Gause/Photo Researchers, Inc.; p. 7 (left): M. I. Walker/Photo Researchers, Inc.; pp. 7 (right), 11 (left), 37: Cabisco/Visuals Unlimited; p. 8: Paul Shambroom/Photo Researchers, Inc.; p. 9: Photo Researchers, Inc.; pp. 11 (right), 15, 28 (top right): CNRI/SPL/Photo Researchers, Inc.; p. 12 (left): Kevin Collins/Visuals Unlimited; p. 12 (right): Ray Ellis/Photo Researchers, Inc.; p. 14: IBMRL/Visuals Unlimited; pp. 17, 22: A. B. Dowsett/SPL/Photo Researchers, Inc.; p. 18 (left): K. G. Murti/Visuals Unlimited; p. 18 (right): Hans Gelderblom/Visuals Unlimited; p. 19 (top): M. Wurtz/Biozentrum, Univ. of Basel/Photo Researchers, Inc.; p. 19 (bottom): Wayside/Visuals Unlimited; p. 21: T. E. Adams/Visual Unlimited; p. 25: NIBSC/SPL/Photo Researchers, Inc.; p. 27: Carl O. Wirsen/Visuals Unlimited; p. 28 (left): Gopal Murti/Photo Researchers, Inc.; p. 28 (bottom right): Omikron/Science Source/Photo Researchers, Inc.; p. 31: E. R. Degginger; p. 33: Michael Gabridge/Visuals Unlimited; p. 35: Biophoto Associates/Photo Researchers, Inc.; p. 36: Gregory Ochoki/Photo Researchers, Inc.; p. 41: M. Abbey/Visuals Unlimited; p. 44 (top): R. Oldfield/Visuals Unlimited; p. 44 (bottom): G. Tortoli/Photo Researchers, Inc.; p. 46: Eric Grave/Science Source/Photo Researchers, Inc.; p. 48: L. West/Photo Researchers, Inc.; p. 49: H. W. Johansen/Visuals Unlimited; p. 51: D. P. Wilson/Eric and David Hosking/Photo Researchers, Inc.; p. 52: David M. Phillips/Visuals Unlimited; p. 53: Jan Hinsch/Photo Researchers, Inc.

CONTENTS

— · — · — · — · — · —

THE KINGDOMS OF LIFE

ANIMALS

Great horned owl

VERTEBRATES

Day octopus

INVERTEBRATES

PLANTS

Silver vase

FUNGI

Hygrophorus mushroom

MONERANS

Cyanobacteria

PROTISTS

Diatoms

MONERANS and PROTISTS

1

OUR LIVING WORLD

IS SOMEBODY CLASSIFYING *YOU*?

Today's computers can't really think the way people do, but they can store enormous amounts of information, recall it, and perform calculations much faster than humans can. These abilities have made it possible to build up databases of various kinds of information. With the right programming, a computer can sort the information in a database into many different categories and find patterns in the information that would not

A Cray supercomputer can solve complicated numerical problems with great speed.

be easy to spot otherwise. A database for a CD collection, for example, could be used to quickly find the titles of all the songs by a particular composer, or those played by a certain group, or to determine which CD contains a favorite song. Merchants use computers to track store inventories and customer accounts. Each time a person charges something on a credit card, makes a long-distance phone call, subscribes to a magazine, or does any of hundreds of other things, data are added to computer databases. Some people are worried about how all this information could be used. By analyzing the information in databases, for example, someone could find out a lot about your interests and how you live. Legislators are just beginning to think about what laws are needed to protect people's privacy in this computer age.

Have you ever played twenty questions? A person thinks of an object. Then, using general questions to narrow down the possibilities, the other players try to guess what the object is. The first question is usually, "Is it animal, vegetable, or mineral?" This question reflects the way people used to think about the world. For thousands of years philosophers, scientists, and everyone else believed that all solid objects could be placed in one of those three categories. Animals and plants (the "vegetable" category) were the two kingdoms of living things. "Mineral" referred to nonliving objects.

How can you tell if something is alive? In the everyday world it seems obvious. Living things can move, take in raw materials and use them to build their own special chemicals, grow, change (or **mutate**), and reproduce themselves, passing on hereditary changes to their offspring. Some nonliving things can do some of these things, but not all of them. A snowball rolling downhill, for example, moves and grows larger; but it doesn't provide the power for its own movement, and it grows by adding more snow on the outside of the ball, not by taking in raw materials and processing them. If it splits in two, it is not reproducing; it's just breaking into pieces rather than forming little copies of itself.

The distinction between plants and animals seemed just as obvious. Animals can move around (at least at some time in their lives), and they must eat to get the raw materials they need. Plants don't move from place to place (though they can—very slowly—move their leaves, flowers, or other parts), they are usually green, and they make their own food using light energy. When microscopes were invented and scientists discovered that plants and animals are made up of many tiny living units called **cells**, they found other differences. Animal cells, for example, are enclosed in a very thin, flexible covering called a **cell membrane**. Plant cells have a covering membrane, too, but it is surrounded by a rigid, tough **cell wall** made of cellulose.

SORTING IT ALL OUT

Grouping things into categories according to their similarities and differences is a form of **classification**: the process of dividing objects into related groups. **Taxonomy** is the science of classifying or arranging living things into groups based on characteristics they share. It comes from the Greek words *taxis*, which means "arrangement," and *nomos*, which means "law."

Carl Linnaeus (1707–1778) devised the scientific method of naming living things. He wrote books in Latin on the classification of plants and animals.

The classification system biologists use today is based on the one devised by the eighteenth-century Swedish botanist and naturalist Carl Linnaeus. Each living thing is given a two-part name based on some of its most important characteristics. The first name corresponds to a **genus**, a group of rather closely related kinds of organisms. The second name, the **species**, identifies the particular kind of creature within the genus.

FINDING A HOME IN THE SYSTEM

Even before the invention of microscopes opened up a whole new world of life, there were some living things that did not fit comfortably into either the plant or the animal kingdom. Mushrooms, molds, and other fungi are plantlike in many ways, but they are not green and do not make their own food. And their cell walls contain chitin (the substance found in the outer covering of insects) rather than cellulose.

In the microworld there are many more kinds of living organisms that do not seem to fit very well into either the plant or the animal kingdom. Many microorganisms consist of just a single cell. Some of them are very simple creatures, but other single-celled organisms are quite complex indeed. Their tiny bodies contain specialized **organelles** (little organs)—structures that do the same kinds of tasks that the organs of multicelled animals and plants perform. Structures in the tiny pond creature paramecium, for example, are like a mouth and throat; other organelles digest food and eliminate wastes, and tiny hairlike cilia, like fringes of eyelashes on the outer surface, beat back and forth to propel the paramecium through the water.

Many of the single-celled organisms have some of the characteristics of typical plants or typical animals, but not all of the characteristics. Some of them have characteristics of both plants and animals. Scientists called these organisms **protozoans**, which means "first animals." Traditionally they were placed in the animal kingdom in the phylum Protozoa.

In 1866 Ernst H. Haeckel, a German zoologist, suggested that certain kinds of organisms belonged in a third kingdom, which he called **Protista**. Haeckel included a variety of living things in this kingdom, including fungi and sponges. Today there is still disagreement about how many kingdoms living things should be divided into and which organisms belong in which kingdom.

Biologists usually classify living things into five kingdoms: monerans, protists, fungi, plants, and animals. But even these biologists disagree about which organisms belong in these groups, particularly in the kingdom Protista. Some biologists include among the **protists** some fungi, certain kinds of seaweed, and other multicellular or-

Silly sentences can help you remember lists. The first letters of

Killer **P**rotists **C**rawl **O**n **F**uzzy **G**reen **S**lides

can help you remember the major groups of the scientific classification system:

Kingdom, **P**hylum, **C**lass, **O**rder, **F**amily, **G**enus, **S**pecies.

In the kingdom Protista the animal-like creatures are grouped into phyla. But the plantlike protists, such as algae, used to belong to the plant kingdom, which is grouped into divisions. Taxonomists usually follow the older rules and call the largest groups of algae divisions. Bacteria, which form the kingdom Monera, also used to be thought of as plants. Therefore, many classification experts use the term *divisions* for the major groups of bacteria as well.

Each successive group in the classification contains a smaller number of organisms that are more closely related to one another.

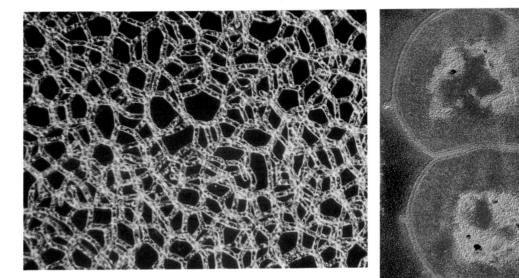

Green algae (above) *are plantlike protists. Bacteria* Streptococcus viridans (right) *are monerans.*

ganisms whose cells are not specialized to perform particular functions. Others, however, include only single-celled organisms that have a **nucleus** (the control center of a cell) and certain organelles. Single-celled organisms without an organized nucleus and typical organelles are grouped in the kingdom **Monera**.

2

DISCOVERING A
TINY NEW WORLD

In 1676 a Dutch lens maker named Antonie van Leeuwenhoek used a magnifying lens to look at a drop of pond water. He was amazed to see tiny creatures wriggling around in the water. He checked other things, such as saliva and a drop of sewer water, and saw these tiny creatures in every sample he checked. Leeuwenhoek knew these creatures were alive because of the way they moved. He called them "animalcules" and "wee beasties."

As the years went by, other scientists used better magnifying tools to look at the creatures that inhabited this hidden world all around them. But these creatures were a real mystery for the scientists. Where did they come from and what did they do? Many believed that these tiny living things came from nonliving things, just as they believed that fly maggots came from rotting meat. This idea is called **spontaneous generation**.

Compare an early microscope (far left) to a modern scanning electron microscope (left), which can magnify a specimen up to 500,000 times.

Most people believed in spontaneous generation until the 1860s, when French scientist Louis Pasteur showed that these tiny creatures—called microbes (from *micro* meaning "small" and *bios* for "life")—did not mysteriously arise from foods or dead things. Instead, microbes reproduced to produce new microbes, and they traveled through the air on tiny specks of dust. Pasteur showed that boiling soup broth kills any creatures living in it. If the container is properly sealed so that microbes are not allowed to get inside, the boiled broth remains sterile (free of living creatures). But when the broth is cooled and exposed to ordinary air, tiny microbes will begin to grow in it. Pasteur's discovery led to the theory that life can only arise from living things. This concept is called **biogenesis**.

HOW DID LIFE BEGIN?

Scientists believe that life arose on our planet about four billion years ago. But if living things can only come from other living things, then where did the first living thing come from? Scientists think that the world was once very different than it is today. They have evidence that before life arose, earth's atmosphere was made up of different gases, including hydrogen, methane, ammonia, and water vapor. We could not live under these conditions, but they may have been just right for life to have evolved.

In the 1950s scientists conducted an experiment to see whether they could reconstruct what might have happened. Hydrogen, methane, water vapor, and ammonia gases were combined in a sterile container. Sparks, which would be like bolts of lightning in earth's primitive conditions, were passed through the mixture. Several days later the scientists discovered that amino acids—the building blocks of proteins—had formed. Proteins are the building materials of all living things.

Scientists believe that the oceans and ponds of primitive earth were filled with amino acids that had formed under similar conditions. As the amino acids floated about, they bumped into one another. Sometimes they stuck together, forming larger and larger molecules. Scientists have been able to produce proteinlike substances in the laboratory from simple amino acids. The primitive earth itself was like a giant laboratory. Over billions of years many kinds of molecules were formed. Some of these were able to make copies of themselves. A molecule would divide in half when it reached a certain size. Each half was identical to the other, and each continued to "grow" by joining with the right amino acids until it was ready to divide, too.

Many kinds of molecules were formed, but only the ones that were able to **replicate** (make copies of themselves) were made over and over. The molecules that arose

DNA as seen through a scanning tunneling electron microscope. Such a microscope can allow us to see surface atoms.

were not yet "alive." But these self-replicating molecules developed into more and more complex molecules, ultimately forming RNA and DNA. DNA (deoxyribonucleic acid) contains the instructions for making proteins. Portions of these instructions are copied out in molecules of RNA, which is like a pattern or template on which proteins form. Amino acids floating around attach to the right spots on the RNA, producing a new protein.

How did these building blocks come together to create something that was alive? No one is exactly sure, but scientists have several theories.

WHAT IS LIFE?

An even more basic question is, What does it mean for something to be alive? It is often obvious that something is alive (such as a purring cat) and something else isn't (a rock). But sometimes it isn't as clear-cut. A **virus**, for example, is made up of a DNA or RNA molecule surrounded by a protein coat. If it is placed in the proper conditions, it causes living things to make more of itself. But it can't exist on its own. Is it alive?

Although there is a lot of debate on the subject, most scientists consider a cell to be the smallest structure of something that is alive. It is an enclosed system that takes in food, water, and gases; gets rid of wastes; reacts to changes in the environment; and can grow and make more of itself. According to these conditions, a virus isn't alive. But it may be an important link between the highly complex molecules that evolved on the primitive earth and the first simple living things.

One of the most obvious differences between a cell and a virus is that a cell has a cell membrane surrounding fluids and various organelles. And yet, even a virus has a protein coat around its DNA or RNA. At some point, self-replicating molecules formed protein or lipid (fatty) coats around themselves. This may have occurred when a molecule was trapped inside a membrane that formed on its own. (You can see for yourself how membranes form when you place a drop of dishwashing detergent in water—see

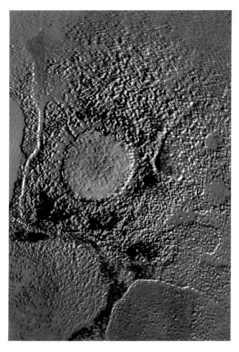

A micrograph of a single virus particle of cytomegalovirus, showing its DNA in the center (pale green) surrounded by a large protein coat (orange)

all the filmy bubbles that form.) Molecules that were trapped in certain kinds of membranes were able to grow and divide better. (The contents inside the membrane can be very different from the contents outside.)

As we study monerans, protists, and other microbes in the chapters that follow, we will see that these organisms provide evidence for scientists to explain how all of the parts of a living cell evolved.

3

AT LIFE'S BORDERLINE

The first step toward discovering viruses was taken in 1892 when a Russian botanist named Dmitri Ivanovsky tried to figure out what was causing a disease that produced spots on tobacco leaves. Extracts from infected leaves transferred the disease to healthy plants. But the finest filters available could not filter out any bacteria or other germs. Slowly scientists learned more about the tiny disease causers. It was not until 1939 that a virus was actually seen, using an electron microscope. (It was the same tobacco mosaic virus that started the story.)

WHAT IS A VIRUS?

Unlike all living things in the five-kingdom classification system, viruses are not cells, nor are they made of cells. Of all the requirements for life, viruses satisfy only two: they can reproduce and mutate, and they can do these things only when they are inside a living cell. Viruses infect the cells of all kinds of living things: animals, plants, fungi, protists, and bacteria.

When a virus is outside of its host cell, it is called a **virion**. A virion is made of a core of genetic material—either DNA or RNA, but not both. Around the core is a protein coat, and that in turn may be enclosed in a more complex covering called an **envelope**. The largest viruses, such as smallpox and vaccinia (cowpox) viruses, are actually big enough to be seen with an optical microscope, although they were not recognized at first. Vaccinia virus is about 300 by 200 by 100 nanometers large. (A nanometer is 0.000001 millimeter, or 0.00000004 inch.) Tobacco mosaic virus is rod-shaped, 250 nanometers by 18 nanometers. The poliovirus is about 30 nanometers in diameter. (To give you an idea of just how small viruses are—if humans were the size of polioviruses, one million people standing in line would measure a little more than an inch!)

Viruses "come alive" only when they infect a cell. They reproduce by taking over the host cell's protein-making equipment. The viral genetic material instructs the host to manufacture new viruses out of materials the host takes in. Some viruses kill their host cells, which burst open, releasing new virus particles. Others can coexist relatively peacefully with their hosts, even inserting their viral genetic material into the host's own genes. Medical researchers believe that many cancerous tumors are caused by genes from tumor viruses, which may remain quietly within the cells for generations until something "turns them on" and sparks a mad process of uncontrolled growth.

Vaccinia virus particles magnified 17,500 times appear as brick-shaped structures.

Most viruses are rather choosy about their hosts and can infect only one particular living species or a group of somewhat similar species. Some animal viruses are surrounded by a membrane that was made from the previous host's materials. This membrane can then join with a similar membrane of a new cell. Scientists believe that viruses arose when pieces of genetic material "escaped" from a particular kind of cell. Using genetic tests, scientists have found that viruses are more similar to the cells they infect than to other viruses.

SORTING OUT THE VIRUSES

Hundreds of virus species have been observed, and more are being discovered all the time. (There are more than a hundred viruses, of several different species, that cause the common cold!) Scientists use many observations to classify viruses. The shape of the virus is an important clue. Some viruses are shaped like coiled springs, others are many-faceted like tiny gemstones; some have protein tails that make them look like tiny tennis rackets. Another classification clue is what host they infect. Other deciding factors include whether their genetic material is DNA or RNA, and whether the virus is surrounded by an envelope.

Many viruses are carried by insects and other arthropods. The carrier is not affected, but serious diseases can result when a human or other mammal is bitten.

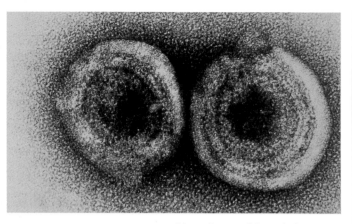
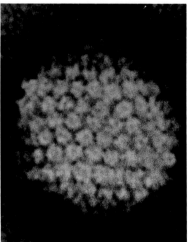

Retroviruses (above) *resemble coiled springs.*
Adenoviruses (right) *look like faceted gems.*

THEY MULTIPLIED LIKE RABBITS

In 1859 some homesick settlers in Australia imported rabbits from Europe. The rabbits quickly multiplied and became pests, competing with livestock for food. Nearly a century later, scientists got the bright idea of introducing the myxoma virus, a relative of the flu virus, which is spread by mosquitoes. In South America, where it originated, this virus causes a mild disease (myxomatosis) in forest rabbits, but it is 99 percent fatal to infected European rabbits.

Everyone expected that soon nearly all the Australian rabbits would be wiped out by the deadly disease. But two things happened. The few rabbits that survived the disease multiplied and had offspring who were also resistant to myxomatosis. And the virus began to change to milder forms that did not kill as quickly and thus had more time to spread to new hosts. Within seven years the virus epidemics were killing only 25 percent of the infected rabbits, and the rabbits began to multiply again. Now, with the Australian rabbit population close to 300 million, scientists are trying once more, with a virus that causes a deadly respiratory infection in rabbits and first appeared in China in 1984.

Scientists discovered a lot about viruses in general and about genetics by studying viruses that infect **bacteria**. They are called **bacteriophages**, which means "bacteria eaters." Bacteriophages are among the most complicated viruses (many have a tail attached to the head and fibers from the tail that attach the virus to a bacterium), but they are very easy to "grow" in the laboratory inside bacteria.

Most bacteriophages contain DNA. The genetic material of most viruses that infect plants is RNA, but the group of animal viruses includes both DNA and RNA species.

This T4 bacteriophage is a virus that infects only bacteria. It attaches to a bacterium by means of its spidery tail fibers.

Animal DNA viruses include a number of important families:

Poxviruses (large oval-shape) that cause smallpox and cowpox

Herpesviruses (medium to large with an envelope) that cause cold sores, genital herpes, chicken pox, mononucleosis

Adenoviruses (medium-sized) that cause respiratory infections, sore throats, tonsillitis, conjunctivitis, and intestinal infections

Papovaviruses (small) that cause warts, brain diseases, and genital cancers

The families of animal RNA viruses include the following:

Picornaviruses (small) include polioviruses, rhinoviruses that are the main causes of the common cold, and viruses that cause inflammation of the brain (their name comes from *pico*, meaning "small," and *RNA*)

Togaviruses (medium-sized surrounded by an envelope) are often transmitted by insects and other arthropods and include yellow fever and rubella (German measles) viruses

Orthomyxoviruses (medium-sized, often with spikes) cause influenza

Paramyxoviruses (large, often with spikes) cause mumps, and distemper in dogs

Retroviruses cause AIDS and some types of cancer

In plants, viruses can be spread by insects such as aphids, or they may come from infected seeds. These viruses cause spots or streaks or patterns on flowers, fruits, and leaves, or cause an infected plant to be smaller or produce less fruit. Some of the prize tulip varieties, with striped or patterned petals, are infected with harmless plant viruses.

The streaking in this type of tulip is caused by a harmless plant virus.

4

−·−·−·−·−

THE FIRST LIVING CELLS

−·−·−·−·−

There are more bacteria on our planet than any other type of living organism. (In fact, there are more bacteria in your mouth right now than the number of people who have ever lived!) So in some ways bacteria are the most successful life-form ever to exist.

OLDEST, SIMPLEST, AND MOST SUCCESSFUL

Bacteria have been around for a long, long time. In fact, bacteria are the oldest known life-forms on our planet. (The oldest fossils of living things that have been discovered are bacteria that lived 3½ billion years ago.) Many scientists believe that all of the life on our planet today evolved from bacteria ancestors. They think that protists evolved from bacteria, and then the fungi, plants, and animals evolved from protists. Even viruses, which are much simpler than bacteria, are believed to have arisen later. Bacteria ruled the earth for more than 2 billion years. During that time they adapted to spread into nearly every habitat.

Bacteria are among the simplest and smallest of all living things. Most bacteria are from 0.000012 to 0.00008 inch (that is, 0.3 to 2.0 micrometers) long; 0.035 ounce (1 gram) of soil may contain 2.5 billion bacteria. In the past, these single-celled organisms were usually classified in the plant kingdom, but some scientists classified them with other single-celled creatures in the kingdom Protista. Today, most scientists classify bacteria and **cyanobacteria** (once called blue-green algae) in their own kingdom, Monera.

Monerans are different from all other living things. They are **prokaryotes**—they do not have a nucleus surrounded by a membrane. (The prefix *pro-* means "before," and the

Greek word *karyon* means "nucleus.") Single-celled organisms that do have a nucleus surrounded by a membrane are called **eukaryotes**. (The prefix *eu-* means "true.")

Although bacteria don't have a real nucleus, they do have a nuclear area that contains DNA, the genetic material found in all living things. This substance contains the instructions to make new organisms. It also helps control the cell's growth and reproduction. Bacterial chromosomes are arranged in a circular loop and contain only DNA; the chromosomes of eukaryotes are usually long chains of DNA, associated with proteins. Monerans are different from the rest of the living world in other ways, too. They do not have many of the organelles that are found in other living cells. And although most bacteria, like plants, have a cell wall surrounding the cell membrane, bacterial cell walls contain substances that are not found in plants or other living things.

Anabaena spiroides *are an example of spiral-shaped cyanobacteria, as you might have guessed from the name.*

CRACKING THE CODE

The DNA that makes up the genes of bacteria and other organisms consists of long chains of chemicals called **nitrogen bases**. There are four main kinds of bases in DNA: A, C, G, and T; and thus the genetic instructions are spelled out in a four-letter alphabet. In 1995 researchers announced that they had worked out the complete sequences of bases in the chromosomes of a bacterium, *Hemophilus influenzae*, and a mycoplasma, *Mycoplasma genitalium*. They hope to use this knowledge to make better vaccines and drugs.

ECONOMY-MODEL CELLS

All bacteria have a stretchy baglike wrapping that surrounds the cell. This cell membrane contains tiny pores or openings that allow small molecules of food to pass into the cell. Large molecules cannot fit through the pores. Inside the cell is a jellylike substance called **cytoplasm**. Cytoplasm holds the nuclear body that contains the bacterium's genetic instructions as well as many kinds of enzymes (special chemicals that help build different parts of the cell, and also break down food). Nearly all bacteria also have a cell wall

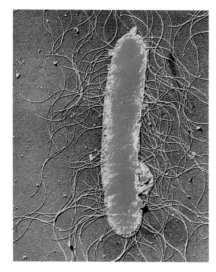

Proteus mirabilis, shown here magnified 6,000 times, has many flagella to propel it. It is normally present in human intestines.

around the cell membrane. This is a tough layer that protects the bacterium. Some bacteria also have another protective layer called a **capsule**. This slimy layer, wrapped around the cell wall, protects the bacterium from harmful chemicals.

In many species, hairlike structures called **flagella** extend through the layers and help the bacterium to move. These flagella are very different from those of other single-celled organisms. A bacterium's flagellum is just a single fiber; the flagella of other living things are much more complicated. Also, instead of whipping back and forth as other flagella do, a bacterium's flagellum rotates at the place where it is connected to the cell, working like a ship's propeller to push the bacterium along.

MONERANS ARE EVERYWHERE

Some monerans live alone, others in groups or clusters called **colonies**. Individual moneran cells can be seen only with a microscope, but some colonies contain so many cells that we can see them clearly without any magnification.

Monerans can live in a wide range of environments—almost everywhere, even where no other life can survive. For example, cyanobacteria—also called blue-green bacteria—can be found in frozen wastelands and in hot springs. Many monerans live in environments without oxygen. They can live on a wider variety of foods than other living things. Free-living bacteria are found in soil and water, and parasitic bacteria are

SURVIVAL CHAMPIONS

Some bacteria form a resting stage when they can't find enough food, or when there isn't enough oxygen or water, or when it is too hot or too cold. A thicker cell membrane forms beneath the normal cell membrane, and the bacteria become inactive until conditions are better. A **bacterium** in this state is called a **bacterial spore**. Bacterial spores can resist extremely harsh conditions. Some can survive after being boiled for hours or frozen for centuries. The spores change back into active bacteria when conditions are right again. Bacterial spores that survived for two thousand years in the bodies of Egyptian mummies and then caused disease were the basis for legends of "the mummy's curse."

found in nearly all multicelled plants and animals. Air and water currents can carry bacteria long distances. Bacteria are also carried on objects such as eating utensils and clothing. Right now there are many kinds of bacteria living peacefully on your skin and in your respiratory and digestive systems.

Most bacteria feed on dead organisms. Some are parasites of various kinds of organisms. Many parasitic bacteria cause very little or no harm, but others cause serious diseases. Some bacteria make their own food. Others can either make their own food or take in nutrients, depending on the conditions.

MAKING MORE BACTERIA

Bacteria usually reproduce by splitting into two identical bacteria. This asexual reproduction is called **binary fission**, and the two new bacteria are called daughter cells. Most bacteria reproduce very quickly—some kinds reproduce every twenty minutes! A single bacterium can multiply into a billion bacteria in only ten hours if there is enough food. When a bacterium splits into two cells, the DNA material in the two daughter cells is exactly the same as that of the parent. But in some species a bacterium can also exchange DNA material with another bacterium through a tube that connects the two. This process, called **conjugation**, is a kind of sexual reproduction. One bacterium is considered a male cell and the other a female cell. Some bacteria can also take pieces of DNA from dead bacterial cells.

BACTERIA ARE IMPORTANT

We think of bacteria as "germs," and a few do cause diseases. But most bacteria do not harm humans or other living creatures. Some are even helpful. Certain bacteria in your intestines help to destroy other organisms that could be harmful. Others aid in digestion or make vitamins that your body needs.

Bacteria play an important part in the balance of nature. They are among nature's best recyclers. Bacteria and fungi help to break down animal wastes and organisms that have died. In this way chemical elements such as carbon and nitrogen are returned to the water or soil so that other living things can use them. If these elements weren't recycled, not only would living things not be able to find the nutrients they need to live and grow, but the earth would be covered with wastes and dead plants and animals! Other bacteria help plants by changing chemical elements such as nitrogen into compounds that plants can use.

Bacteria also play a vital role in science and industry. They are used to make cheeses and other products such as vinegar, and in sewage systems to break down wastes. Many prescription drugs are made using bacteria, and a bacterium called *Bacillus thuringiensis*, which infects insects, is widely used to control harmful insect pests.

Because bacteria reproduce very quickly, scientists can grow large quantities of them to study. Recently researchers have learned to transfer genes from other species—even humans—to bacteria and use them to produce valuable proteins. Human growth hormone, for example, can be used to treat certain kinds of growth disorders, allowing children who would have been dwarfs to grow to a normal height. At one time this protein was obtained from the pituitary glands in the brains of people who had died. One hundred pituitary glands were needed to get enough of the hormone to treat one child for a year! Now that human growth hormone can be produced in large amounts by genetically engineered bacteria, reproducing in huge vats, the treatment of growth disorders has become practical.

TROUBLEMAKERS

Bacteria cause many different diseases in humans, such as cholera, gonorrhea, leprosy, Lyme disease, pneumonia, syphilis, tuberculosis, typhoid fever, and whooping cough. These bacteria get into the body through a break in the skin or through one of the body openings, such as the nose or mouth. They destroy healthy cells, preventing the body from working properly. Other kinds of harmful bacteria produce poisons called toxins that are harmful to humans. These cause diseases such as botulism, diphtheria, scarlet fever, and tetanus. Bacteria also cause diseases in other animals and plants. Soft rot decays fruits and vegetables, for example.

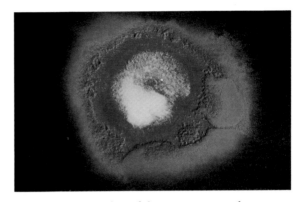

This virus, a member of the Paramyxoviridae family, causes mumps in humans.

WAR AGAINST BACTERIA

Our skin and the membranes that line our respiratory and digestive tracts help to keep most harmful bacteria from getting into the body. When they do get inside, the body goes into action to destroy them. White blood cells travel through the bloodstream to "gobble up" bacteria. The body produces antibodies to weaken or kill foreign organisms. Some antibodies protect us from the toxins produced by bacteria.

Scientists may use weakened or dead bacteria to make **vaccines**. A vaccine causes the body to make antibodies against a certain kind of bacteria. If we are ever exposed to that kind of bacteria, the body will be ready to fight it off. When bacteria make us sick, a doctor may prescribe a drug called an **antibiotic**. Antibiotics kill or weaken bacteria so that our bodies can get the problem under control.

When you get a scrape or cut, you clean it with a chemical called an **antiseptic** to keep bacteria from getting inside your body. Household cleaners contain chemicals called **disinfectants** to kill bacteria, and we use hot water to wash dishes and clothes because heat kills bacteria. Bacteria are also killed in the normal cooking process.

5

AN UNFINISHED CLASSIFICATION

Under a microscope many bacteria look very similar in size and shape, but they are often very different from one another. Scientists believe that the bacteria alive today have come from a number of different evolutionary ancestors. These separate lines have been following their own evolutionary paths for billions of years. Since bacteria have evolved to live in practically every environment, they have many different structures and lifestyles. This makes it very difficult for taxonomists to classify them.

Because of these difficulties, the classification of monerans has not followed the pattern for the other kingdoms of life. Just like other organisms, individual kinds of bacteria have traditionally been assigned a species and genus, but the next level has often been division or phylum; organisms in the other kingdoms belong to a specific class, order, and family as well. More-powerful microscopes and sophisticated methods of chemical analysis are now making it possible to trace relationships and fill in some of the blanks. But there is still no full agreement on the details of bacterial taxonomy, and competing classifications divide the monerans into different numbers of divisions.

HIGHER THAN A KINGDOM?

Where do we begin? Some bacteria are so unlike others that they have to be placed into two separate groups. In fact, some scientists think the classification system should include a level higher than kingdom in order to best show bacterial relationships. They think that all living things can be divided into one of three domains: domain **Eucarya** includes eukaryotes (protists, fungi, plants, and animals); domain **Archaea** includes one group of bacteria called archaebacteria ("ancient bacteria"); and domain **Bacteria** includes the other group of bacteria, called **eubacteria** ("true bacteria"). Other scientists place the archaebacteria and the true bacteria in separate kingdoms, making a total of six kingdoms of living things.

To simplify matters, in this book we have placed all bacteria within the kingdom Monera. We have then divided the thousands of kinds of bacteria into two main groups: archaebacteria and true bacteria.

Archaebacteria live in environments without oxygen—in fact, they are killed when exposed to oxygen. Many of them live in hydrothermal vents, volcanic openings in the deep-sea floor. They make their own food, using simple substances such as sulfur, hydrogen, and carbon dioxide. Their cell walls are not like those of any other living creatures, and their genetic material is arranged very differently.

True bacteria include most monerans. Their genetic material is arranged in a way similar to that of the eukaryotes. Most bacteria are **heterotrophs**, which means they cannot make their own food. They must get the nutrients they need by taking in organic materials (materials that come from living things). The **autotrophs** make their own food and get their energy either from the sun or from nonorganic materials. (Cyanobacteria, which are autotrophs, use a type of chlorophyll, a pigment that plants use for photosynthesis, but other bacteria use different methods.) Because the two types of true bacteria are so different from each other, scientists believe the lines split early in the development of life-forms.

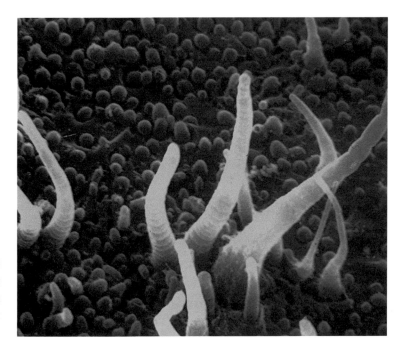

A microbial mat has formed on the surface of a mussel living near a hydrothermal vent in the Galápagos Islands.

SORTING THEM OUT

Dividing the 2,700 species of bacteria into two main groups is helpful, but these groups contain bacteria that are very different from one another. Dividing bacteria by their shape is the simplest way to classify them further. Bacteria can be divided into four groups according to shape. Rod-shaped bacteria are called **bacilli**; round bacteria are called **cocci**; spiral-shaped bacteria are called **spirilla**; and bacteria that look like bent rods are called **vibrios**. (Some classifications include vibrios among the rod-shaped bacteria.)

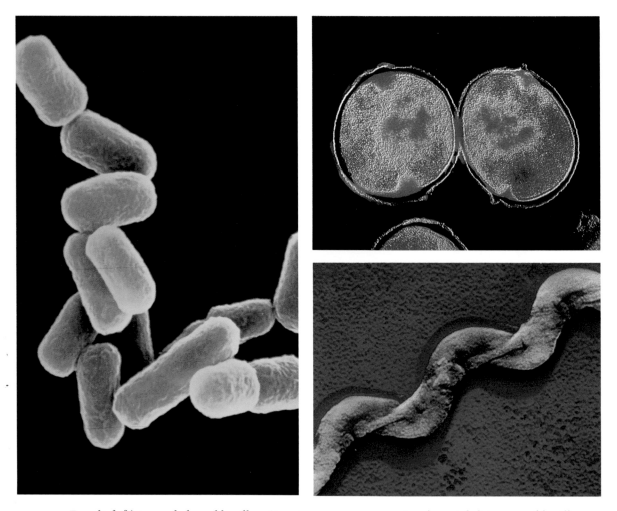

E. coli (left) *is a rod-shaped bacillus,* Streptococcus pneumoniae (top right) *is a round bacillus, and* Leptospira (bottom right) *is a spiral-shaped bacillus. They are shown here greatly magnified.*

The names of bacteria are often formed using one of these group names and adding a prefix that describes the way the bacteria link together: *diplo* describes a pair of bacteria, *staphylo* is a cluster, and *strepto* is a chain. For example, the bacteria that cause strep throat are round bacteria that form chains, so their genus is called *Streptococcus*. Staphylococci cluster and cause many serious infections. The bacterium that causes tuberculosis grows in filaments similar to the way fungi grow and is called *Mycobacterium tuberculosis* because *myco* is the Greek word for "fungus."

Other factors considered in classifying bacteria include type of movement, the way they take in food, whether or not they form spores, whether they have cell walls, and the components of the cell wall.

FINE-TUNING

As scientists developed better tools for studying bacteria, they found that even bacteria with similar shapes seemed to be quite different from one another. By studying the genetic material and the biochemical reactions that go on in the bacteria, scientists could figure out which are more closely related. The most closely related bacteria have a great deal of genetic material in common. Those with more differences in their DNA belong to lines that split off earlier from a common ancestor.

Biologists use different rules to divide the two major groups of bacteria. Archaebacteria are grouped into three main phyla (some biologists call these groups divisions instead of phyla) according to the habitats they live in. **Thermoacidophiles** live in hot places, **methanogens** produce methane gas, and **strict halophiles** live in very salty environments.

The true bacteria are divided into three main phyla based on their cell walls. In 1884 a Danish physician and bacteriologist, Hans Christian Gram, developed a complicated staining system, using two different dyes, that distinguishes between bacteria with two types of cell walls. **Gram-negative** bacteria stain pink to red; **gram-positive** species stain blue or purple. The third phylum is made up of **mycoplasmas**, which have no cell walls.

SPOTLIGHT ON ARCHAEBACTERIA

Thermoacidophile means "heat- and acid-loving." These bacteria can live in extremely hot places such as hot springs. One species, *Sulfolobus*, dies when the temperature drops to 131°F (55°C)! The hot sulfur springs where these bacteria live are also extremely acidic; most organisms cannot survive in this habitat. The extreme environmental conditions in which archaebacteria live are similar to those that were common when life first arose; today such conditions are found only in rare places.

Ten species of bacteria belong to a group called methanogens because they produce methane as a by-product when they use energy. All of the methane in our air comes from these bacteria; they release about 2 billion tons of methane gas each year! A methanogen called *Methanopyrus* lives at the bottom of the ocean near vents of undersea volcanoes, where the temperature rises to 270°F (132°C).

The strict halophiles ("salt lovers") contain a pink coloring and grow only in extremely salty conditions where few other organisms could survive. Halophiles have been found living in lakes that were as alkaline as household ammonia.

TRUE BACTERIA CLOSE-UP

After dividing the true bacteria into three main phyla, they are further subdivided based on shape and other properties. Here are some of the main types:

Gram-negative bacteria: About three-quarters of the true bacteria are gram-negative. They include

- **Gliding bacteria,** which form filaments or rods that move by gliding along on a trail of slime. They are also unusual because they form branched structures called fruiting bodies. In plants, seeds are produced inside fruits. Spores are produced inside the gliding bacteria's fruiting bodies. These spores are thick-walled and can survive in harsh environments.

- **Spirochetes,** which are coiled into spirals and move with flagella. Many are parasites in humans, such as the bacteria that cause the sexually transmitted disease syphilis and those responsible for Lyme disease.

- **Gram-negative rods** (or bacilli): This group is very large, and its members are probably not all closely related. Some, such as *Rhizobium*, are important in helping to "fix" nitrogen—that is, change nitrogen gas from the atmosphere into a form plants can use. One of the most studied bacteria of all is *Escherichia coli*, which is a gram-negative rod commonly found in human intestines. This group

This large growth on the tree trunk is called a crown gall. It is caused by the bacterium Agrobacterium tumefaciens.

of bacilli also includes many bacteria that cause serious diseases, such as plague (*Yersinia pestis*), cholera (*Vibrio cholerae*), and a common type of food poisoning (*Salmonella typhimurium*). *Agrobacterium tumefaciens* is a bacterium that causes massive tumorlike growths, called crown galls, on trees.

- **Gram-negative cocci**: The best known is the bacterium *Neisseria gonorrhoeae*, which causes the sexually transmitted disease gonorrhea.

- **Rickettsias** and **Chlamydias**: Scientists once grouped rickettsias with viruses because they are so tiny and reproduce only when they are inside a cell. These minute parasites cause diseases such as typhus, which is carried from one person to another by lice. Rocky Mountain spotted fever is carried by ticks. Chlamydias are often grouped with rickettsias because they are also tiny and can live only inside other cells. These bacteria can cause eye infections, sexually transmitted disease, and pneumonia in humans.

- **Cyanobacteria (blue-green bacteria)** contain chlorophyll and were originally classified as algae, but they are monerans because they do not have a true nucleus or organelles with membranes around them, as eukaryotic cells do. Their genetic material is also more similar to that of bacteria than to the DNA of algae. Some scientists place cyanobacteria with the gliding bacteria because they move around like these bacteria.

Cyanobacteria can live in colonies or as individual cells. The colonies form a wide range of shapes, from flat sheets to balls. Some cyanobacteria coat rocks along the shores of oceans, rivers, and lakes with a dark, slippery slime. Those that live on land form a slimy layer on wet ground. Occasionally, lakes look greenish or blue-green because of the large numbers of blue-green bacteria living there. Some cyanobacteria poison animals such as fish and cattle that drink water contaminated with the bacteria.

Not all of the cyanobacteria are blue-green. In addition to chlorophyll, these organisms contain red and blue pigments. Some may be pinkish, brownish, or black, depending on the combination of pigments.

Gram-positive bacteria include

- **Gram-positive rods**, which are divided into two groups. One group produces thick-walled spores. Important members include the bacterium that causes tetanus (*Clostridium tetani*) and the species that causes the lethal food poisoning called botulism (*Clostridium botulinum*). The botulinum toxin is one of the most poisonous substances ever discovered. *Clostridium botulinum* cannot grow in the presence of oxygen, but it thrives in canned foods that have not been properly sterilized. Even if the canned food is cooked after the can is opened, killing the bacteria, the toxins they produced are still present. This group also includes many species of the genus *Bacillus*, including the bacteria that cause anthrax in sheep and humans. The other subgroup of gram-positive rods includes *Lactobacillus*, which produces lactic acid. This bacterium gives yogurt, pickles, and sauerkraut their familiar taste.

- **Gram-positive cocci**: There are many kinds of gram-positive cocci. Staphylococci are found all over our skin and can cause skin problems such as boils, as well as respiratory and intestinal problems. Some species of *Staphylococcus* produce toxins that are a major cause of food poisoning and cause toxic shock syndrome. Different kinds of streptococci can infect nearly every organ system in our bodies. *Streptococcus mutans* produces acid that forms cavities in teeth.

- **Actinomycetes** were once placed with fungi because they form elaborate branches of filaments that look like fungi. *Mycobacterium tuberculosis*, the TB microbe, is an important member of this group. *Streptomyces* is helpful to humans, though. It produces the antibiotic streptomycin. In fact, most antibiotics come from actinomycetes.

Mycoplasmas, the third main phylum, do not have cell walls and are the smallest living cells ever discovered. They also have less than half the DNA of any other living thing. Scientists think they contain the smallest amount of DNA that is needed to code for the proper functioning of a cell. Most are parasites inside animal and plant cells. Without cell walls, they can take on strange shapes.

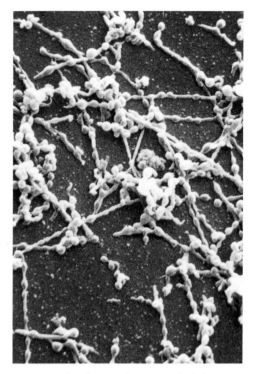

An example of mycoplasmas, which have no cell walls and can take on strange shapes

6

ADVENTURES IN
THE MICROWORLD

Bacteria are prokaryotes; they do not have a nucleus that is surrounded by its own membrane. Eukaryotes are organisms that do have nuclei surrounded by membranes. The nucleus, the cell's control center, contains a complete set of hereditary information in the form of chromosomes. Each chromosome consists of a long strand of DNA, combined with proteins. The cells of eukaryotes also contain many organelles that are not found in prokaryotic organisms. The simplest eukaryotes belong to the kingdom Protista. (Some taxonomists use the alternative name Protoctista.)

WHAT IS A PROTIST?

The only identifying feature common to all protists is that each is surrounded by a membrane. Then the classification becomes more difficult. Many also have cell walls. Some are surrounded by shells that they form around themselves or make from bits of sand. Most protists are single-celled organisms, but they are often very complex. Some protists form colonies, some have more than one nucleus even though they are single-celled, and some are multicellular. The multicellular protists, however, have very simple body forms.

Organisms are placed in the other four kingdoms on the basis of characteristics that they share with the other members of those kingdoms. But Protista is a sort of catchall kingdom for the creatures that do not fit anywhere else; a protist is defined as a eukaryote that is not a fungus, plant, or animal.

Diatoms, for example, have intricate shells that are made of a glasslike material. The two halves of the shell fit together like the top and bottom of a petri dish. Some diatoms can move about, but they have no legs, flagella, or other organs for locomotion. They are not animals, because they photosynthesize like plants. They are not

Microscopic diatoms have glasslike shells containing a nucleus surrounded by a cell membrane.

IS IT A PROTIST OR NOT?

Many biologists use certain criteria to separate protists from other kingdoms:

- Unicellular or colonial organisms are often assigned to kingdom Protista; members of the other kingdoms are usually multicellular.
- Protists are separated from fungi by several criteria: Fungi do not have flagella during any stage of their life cycle. There is no difference between "male" and "female" sex cells (gametes) of fungi. Fungi have chitin in their cell walls.
- Algae develop from a single cell. A plant embryo is protected by tissues formed by the parent plant.
- Many protists ingest (take in) food materials and digest them inside their bodies, as animals do. But animals are multicellular.

plants because (with one exception) they do not have a cell wall made of cellulose. Under the microscope we can see that they are not bacteria because they have a nucleus surrounded by a cell membrane.

Sometimes scientists have a hard time drawing the line between the Protista kingdom and other eukaryotic kingdoms because, since the other organisms arose from protists, there are many overlapping similarities. Animal-like protists are called protozoans. Plantlike protists are called algae. Funguslike protists (including slime molds, chytrids, and water molds) have characteristics shared by members of the fungus kingdom. Therefore, some experts classify them among the fungi.

Most protists are tiny single-celled organisms, but among the multicellular protists are giant kelps, which are one of the longest of all organisms. Some biologists, however, do not consider kelps to be protists and include only single-celled organisms in Protista. These biologists place the multicellular protists with either fungi, plants, or animals.

Scientists are learning about the relationships among the different organisms in the protist kingdom by studying their cell structures with electron microscopes, as well as by methods of molecular biology and biochemistry. Some scientists think that as many as fifty different phyla are needed to classify all of the diverse organisms in this group.

Most protists live in water, either in the oceans, in freshwater, or in the body fluids of other organisms. Some, such as slime molds, live on land in damp soil or in moist decaying trees.

The whole outer surface of a single-celled organism's body is in contact with the watery medium in which it lives. Some protists, like monerans, simply take in the materials they need through their outer membrane, and waste products pass out into the water just as easily. But this kind of life places a limit on the creature's size. If it grows too large, it

Giant kelp growing off the coast of southern California

BLUE-GREENS IN YOUR CELLS?

Scientists believe that many of the organelles in eukaryote cells were originally separate organisms that lived in a symbiotic relationship. Mitochondria, the energy-generating organelles in animal cells, have their own DNA, which is copied separately from that of the chromosomes. The plastids in plant cells, which contain chlorophyll or stored food, also have their own separate DNA.

Both mitochondria and plastids are surrounded by double membranes. The outer membrane is like that of the eukaryotic cell the mitochondrion or plastid inhabits. The inner membrane, however, is like a prokaryotic cell membrane. Scientists have suggested that these organelles started out as free-living bacteria, like today's cyanobacteria, that formed working partnerships with ancient ancestors of animals and plants. Sheltered inside their host cells, they paid for their "lodgings" by producing or converting energy. Cells that used their smaller "guests" as a source of energy instead of digesting them had a better chance to survive, and so the partnership evolved through natural selection.

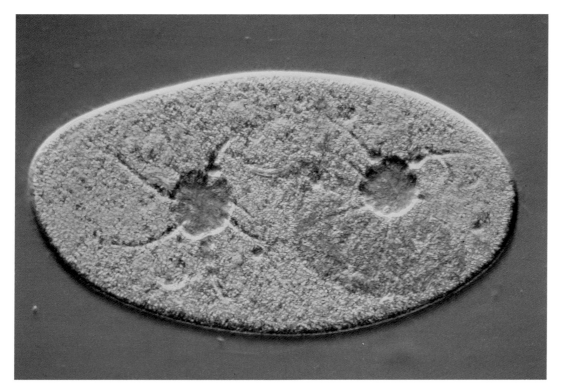

This paramecium contains several contractile vacuoles, which appear as green areas. A paramecium is actually so tiny that it can hardly be seen without a microscope.

will not have enough membrane surface to take care of all of its needs. Special membrane-covered "bags" called vacuoles inside the cell allow some single-celled protists to grow a bit larger. A contractile vacuole bails out excess water in some protists, and food is digested in food vacuoles.

Protists have many ways of getting nutrients. The algae have chlorophyll and get their energy from the sun like plants do. Water molds absorb food as fungi do, and protozoa and slime molds ingest food as animals do.

Many protists live inside other organisms. This relationship is called **endosymbiosis**. For example, the protist *Mixotricha paradoxa* has a number of bacteria living inside it and on its surface. This protist itself lives inside termites, digesting the wood on which they feed. Some protists live in other protists. Radiolarians in the phylum Actinopoda have photosynthetic algae protists living in them; depending on the type of partner, the radiolarian will be greenish or yellowish. Some guests are victims of the host. The host makes use of the products produced in photosynthesis, but the guest gets nothing in return. In other cases the guest receives protection and uses some of the products formed by the host.

THE FIRST EUKARYOTES

Protists probably were the first eukaryotic cells and arose as early as 2.1 billion years ago. Because many kinds of protists have multicellular forms—such as green algae, red algae, and brown algae—and these groups are so different, scientists believe that these algae had different protist ancestors.

Scientists have an idea of how multicelled organisms arose. A type of single-celled green algae, for example, is called *Chlamydomonas*. There are colonial species of green algae that are made up of cells very much like *Chlamydomonas*. The number of cells in the colony differ in various species, ranging from 16 up to 50,000 in the genus *Volvox*. In a large colony, the structures and functions of different cells in the colony begin to become specialized. Patterns such as this suggest that single cells formed colonies, which developed into multicellular organisms.

Scientists think that plants and animals arose from protists. They believe a green alga was the ancestor to plants but are not as sure about fungi and animals. There may have been several different kinds of protists with flagella that developed into different kinds of animals. It is possible that a red alga was the ancestor of fungi.

The phyla of the protist kingdom that we will meet in the following pages include

Sarcodina (amebas)

Actinopoda (radiolarians)

Foraminifera (foraminiferans)

Mastigophora (flagellates)

Ciliophora (ciliates)

Apicomplexa (sporozoans)

Dinoflagellata (dinoflagellates)

Bacillariophyta (diatoms)

Euglenophyta (euglenoids)

Chlorophyta (green algae)

Rhodophyta (red algae)

Phaeophyta (brown algae)

The funguslike protists Myxomycota (plasmodial slime molds), Acrasiomycota (cellular slime molds), and Oomycota (water molds) are considered in the volume on the fungus kingdom.

7

NOT QUITE ANIMALS

Protozoans are single-celled organisms that have many animal-like characteristics. Their name comes from Greek words meaning "first animals." About 40,000 kinds of protozoa have been identified. They are found in moist places—the oceans, freshwater, soil, and inside plants and animals.

Protozoans were first seen in the 1600s. They were classified in the animal kingdom in the phylum Protozoa because of the characteristics that scientists observed. But as scientists studied these microscopic creatures more, they discovered that many had plantlike characteristics as well. Biologists today usually classify them with other simple organisms in the kingdom Protista.

Most protozoans are so small that they can be seen only with a microscope. Scientists measure them in micrometers. (A micrometer is equal to about 0.00004 inch.) The majority of protozoans are about 600 micrometers, but they range between 1 micrometer and 2,000 micrometers long.

Protozoans come in many different shapes, too. Amebas are shapeless blobs; other protozoans have bodies that resemble torpedoes, barrels, cups, and radiating suns. Although they come in different shapes, they are similar in structure. Protozoans have the same basic features as the individual cells that make up the bodies of all multicelled animals. All have a thin outer covering called a cell membrane. Inside the cell, protozoans have organelles, which are specialized structures, each surrounded by its own membrane. These organelles help the protozoan feed, reproduce, and move. The nucleus is the organelle containing the chromosomes, on which the cell's genetic instructions are spelled out in a chemical code in DNA molecules.

Protozoans have lived for millions of years. Over time they have evolved and changed to be able to survive in many different habitats. Some scientists classify proto-

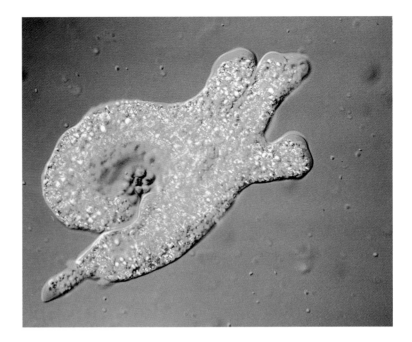

An ameba eats by surrounding its prey and engulfing it.

zoans according to how they reproduce, or the different stages they go through in their life cycles. But most scientists classify protozoans according to the way they move. In such a system there are four groups: flagellates, sarcodines, ciliates, and sporozoans.

Protozoans reproduce very rapidly, a fact that has contributed to their survival over millions of years. Protozoans can reproduce asexually: a cell splits in two, in a process called binary fission. Some parasitic protozoans divide many times inside a host cell. Some protozoans also have forms of sexual reproduction: two cells may fuse together, or two may "mate" and exchange some of their genetic material.

WHIP CRACKERS

The classification of the protists has not yet settled down into any sort of general agreement. So in different books you may find various names for the **flagellates'** phylum, including Flagellata and Zoomastigophora. The prefix *zoo-* means "animal," and *mastigophora* comes from the Greek for "whip bearer"; *flagellum* is Latin for "whip." These protists move by beating long whiplike flagella. (Flagella pull flagellates through the water; they do not push like the tails of tadpoles.) Most flagellates are oval-shaped like chicken eggs. So are most fish and water mammals such as dolphins and whales. Each arrived by evolution at the most streamlined shape for moving in a watery habitat. Their rounded contours offer little resistance, and water flows smoothly along the swimming creatures' sides.

There are 10,000 species in this phylum, making it the largest of the protist phyla. Scientists believe it is also the oldest protist phylum, and some or all of the other protists may have descended from members of this phylum. The Choanoflagellida, one group of zooflagellates (animal-like flagellates), are thought to be the ancestors of the sponges, the most primitive group of animals alive today. Some scientists still include protists such as *Euglena* in the phylum Flagellata, but many place the animal-like and plantlike flagellates in separate phyla.

Certain zooflagellates cause diseases in humans. *Trypanosoma gambiense*, for example, causes sleeping sickness. It is spread by the tsetse fly in Africa. Flies pick up the protozoan when they suck the blood of people infected with this parasite. The trypanosomes multiply in a fly's gut and then migrate to its salivary glands, ready to be injected into the skin of the fly's next victim. After a person is bitten, these single-celled parasites multiply in the blood. Their waste products can build up, causing fever. If they get into the central nervous system, they can cause death.

An intestinal disease called giardiasis is caused by another zooflagellate, *Giardia lamblia*, which is found in contaminated water. In a number of recent incidents, people in various parts of the country have been warned to boil all drinking water after *Giardia* and other disease-causing microbes have been detected in their water sources. (A single child having an attack of diarrhea while swimming in a reservoir can contaminate the water with intestinal parasites.)

Some of the flagellates that live inside the bodies of plants and animals are actually helpful to their hosts. Termites eat wood, for example, but they cannot digest the tough cell walls. Flagellates that live in the termites' guts help to digest the wood so that the termites can get nourishment from it.

THE BLOB FROM PLANET EARTH

Phylum **Sarcodina** contains the **amebas** and their relatives. An ameba is one of the simplest protozoans. It looks like a glob of jelly, but it can move, creeping along on the bottom of a pond (or a microscope slide) by changing the shape of its body. (The name *ameba* comes from a Greek word for "change.") It pushes out its cell membrane to form a sort of fingerlike extension, called a **pseudopod**, which means "false foot." Then the semiliquid contents of the ameba's body flow forward, rounding out the bulge and consolidating its new position.

All amebas are animal-like in the way they eat, and most are predators. They wrap pseudopods around their prey and engulf them. (This process is called phagocytosis, which means "cell eating.") Then the cell membrane closes and traps the prey in a bubble called a food vacuole. Chemicals enter the vacuole and break down the food. The white blood cells that patrol your blood and tissues, hunting down germs and other foreign invaders, look and act very much like amebas.

Some amebas are tiny, some are large—as wide as three pennies stacked on top of one another. Scientists classify different species of amebas by the shape of their pseudopods, whether or not the pseudopods are used for movement and for feeding, and what organelles are present. Most live in freshwater lakes and ponds, but some live in oceans. None have shells.

The ameba may seem to be one of the simplest organisms, but scientists believe that it is not as old, evolutionarily speaking, as other organisms. They think that the sarcodines evolved from more-complex flagellate ancestors. Today there are still examples that show this relationship. *Mastigamoeba aspera* has both pseudopods and flagella. Amebas in the genus *Naegleria*, which can cause a fatal disease in humans, go through two different stages in their life cycle. In one stage they are an ameboid cell, and in the other a flagellated one.

Many ameba-like protozoans live inside the bodies of animals, including humans. Some are harmful, but some aren't. *Entamoeba histolytica* is a harmful ameba, often called dysentery ameba. It is transmitted by eating food or drinking water that is contaminated with sewage, and it causes severe intestinal problems. Other members of this genus live in the intestine, or in the gums around the teeth, and are not harmful.

AMEBAS IN ARMOR

Radiolarians belong to the phylum Actinopoda, which means "ray foot." These protists, found only in the ocean, have ameba-like bodies surrounded by intricate glassy skeletons, through which needlelike pseudopods stick out. Radiolarian skeletons come in many different shapes. The pseudopods help the actinopod float and help to trap food.

Foraminiferans don't look like they are related to amebas. But when they are young, members of the phylum Foraminifera ("hole bearers") are bloblike. Then they secrete a chalklike shell around themselves. As they grow they ooze over the top of the shell and secrete another shell, making a second chamber. Eventually there may be as many as 100 empty chambers around them. They look almost like snail shells with

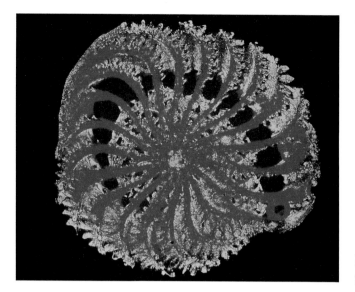

Foraminiferan Elphidium crispum *resembles a spiny snail shell.*

The chalk cliffs of England were formed millions of years ago by deposits of foraminiferan shells. At that time, much of England was underwater.

long thin spines sticking out like a pincushion. The spines are pseudopods, and foraminiferans use these threadlike pseudopods to form a sticky net to capture food.

When foraminiferans die, their shells settle to the ocean floor. There, billions of them form limestone deposits covering millions of square miles, sometimes hundreds of thousands of feet deep. Some beaches are made up of foraminiferan skeletons. Under a microscope you would find about 50,000 foraminiferan shells in every gram of sand.

During different geological periods in earth's history, certain species of foraminiferan shells were abundant. Geologists can use this fact to date other fossils and also to search for oil. (When they find specific types of foraminiferan fossils, they know that oil usually can be found nearby.) Some ancient foraminiferans were huge—about the size of a quarter. Millions of years ago, when much of England was underwater, the chalky shells of foraminiferans formed deposits that we now know as the White Cliffs of Dover.

Today most of the foraminiferan shells that fall to the ocean bottom belong to the family Globigerinidae. One-third of the ocean floor is covered with shells of the genus *Globigerina*.

WAVING EYELASHES

Ciliates (phylum Ciliophora, meaning "eyelash bearers") move by beating tiny cilia that cover their bodies. The cilia are so well coordinated that under a microscope it looks as if they beat in waves. The cell membrane buds inward into the organism to form a food vacuole. This is similar to phagocytosis in amebas.

Ciliates are the most complex protozoans. Many scientists think that they evolved from an ancestor different from that of other protozoa because each organism has more than one nucleus in each cell. (Typically there is one large macronucleus and as many as eighty smaller nuclei, called micronuclei.) This makes ciliates' reproduction very different from the way other protozoa reproduce.

Paramecium is often studied as an example of this phylum. It is slipper-shaped and lives in freshwater. (It is sometimes called the slipper animal.) Thousands of beating cilia move it frontward or backward and sweep food into a groove along the body. *Paramecium* can swim faster than any other protist—faster than 0.08 inch (2 millimeters) per second.

The trumpet-shaped *Stentor* is among the largest of all protozoans. *Vorticella* looks like a long tube with a funnel at the end. It brings food into the funnel by creating a tiny whirlpool at the entrance. One species in this genus, *Vorticella campanula*, is shaped like an upside-down bell. Ciliates in this group are attached to a rock or stick by a stalk secreted by the cell. They live in freshwater and feed on bacteria. When danger is near, they fold in their cilia and the stalk shortens. If conditions are unfavorable, they break away from the stalk and swim to a better location.

Many ciliates can form tough shells around themselves when conditions are not right—when they can't find enough food, or when it is too cold, too hot, or too dry. When conditions are better, they become active again.

Some ciliates have very developed organelles. Some have structures like legs, which are made from cilia that are joined together. These ciliates can walk over surfaces; nervelike fibers coordinate the movement. *Vorticella* has musclelike fibers that help it to quickly pull its stalk away when it is disturbed. *Diplodinium dentatum*, a cili-

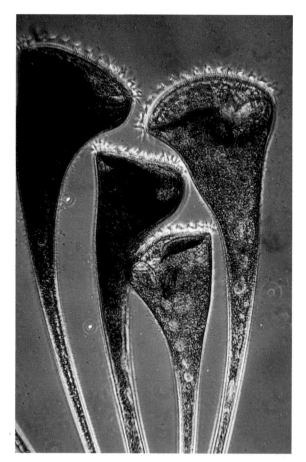

Trumpet-shaped freshwater ciliate Stentor coeruleus. *The cilia around the broad lip of its bell-shaped mouth draws in microscopic bacteria and other food particles.*

ate that lives inside the digestive tracts of cows and other hoofed animals, has all of these traits as well as a "skeleton" and a digestive system consisting of a "mouth," an "esophagus," and an "anus." Fungi, plants, and animals have become complex because of the specialization and coordination of different types of cells. Ciliates were able to develop this kind of complexity by coordinating different kinds of tiny organelles inside a single cell.

STRIPPED DOWN TO THE BASICS

Sporozoans (phylum Sporozoa, now often called Apicomplexa) reproduce using spores, which leads scientists to believe that they are related to slime molds and fungi.

Sporozoans are parasites. Over millions of years, these organisms have evolved in the direction of becoming simpler, losing unnecessary structures. Many have no specific opening to take in food; they absorb nutrients through their cell membrane. They do not move about on their own but are carried inside the body of a host and passed to another host. When sporozoans reproduce, the nucleus divides into many separate nuclei. Fluid from the cell surrounds each nucleus, and each breaks off to form a separate cell. Some sporozoans have a protective coating around them, like seeds.

Many sporozoans need two hosts to complete their life cycle. In one host they reproduce sexually. Then they reproduce asexually in the second host. For example, *Plasmodium*, the parasite that causes malaria, needs both a mosquito and a vertebrate (such as a human) during different stages of its life. *Plasmodium* reproduces in the digestive system of a mosquito. When the mosquito bites a mammal, the one-celled parasites attack the mammal's blood cells. The parasites' waste products, released in the blood, cause fever and chills. Over 300 million people get malaria each year, and more than one million die from it.

8

NOT QUITE PLANTS

When they hear the word *algae*, most people think of the green scum that floats on the surface of a pond or the slippery green film that grows on the inside of an aquarium tank. But algae come in many different forms. Some algae are simple creatures that are found in oceans, lakes, rivers, ponds, and moist soil around the world. Others have become adapted to living in extreme temperatures, such as in frozen polar regions or in steaming hot springs. There are algae that float or swim in the water, while others are attached to stones or plants. Large ocean algae are called seaweed and kelps. (The word *alga* is Latin for "seaweed.") Relatives of freshwater algae live on trees or plants on land. A few even live on animals, such as on turtle shells or sloth fur, and others live inside plants and animals. Certain algae have special partnerships with fungi. They live together and form a single mosslike organism called a lichen.

Tiny lichens called British soldiers (Cladonia cristella) may be found in Michigan.

WHAT'S THE DIFFERENCE BETWEEN AN ALGA AND A PLANT?

Some algae are many-celled and resemble plants, but the way they develop is very different. The zygote of an alga—the product of male and female cells that starts off the life of a new individual—has no protection. A plant zygote is surrounded by tissues supplied by the parent, which provide protection and food as the embryo germinates. Another key difference is in the cell wall. Only the green algae have a cell wall made of cellulose, as plants do.

Like plants, all algae contain chlorophyll. This special green substance allows plants to turn carbon dioxide from the air and water into food, using the energy from sunlight. Animals can't make their own food, so plants, algae, and other food producers play a very important role in the balance of nature. Algae are a major source of food for fish and other animals that live in water.

A by-product of photosynthesis, oxygen, is even more vital to life. When our planet first formed, there was no free oxygen in the air. Now about 20 percent of the gas in our atmosphere is oxygen—all of it produced by the activity of algae and plants. Algae account for more than half of all the photosynthesis on the present-day earth.

Pollution is harmful to many living creatures, but some kinds of algae grow best in waters that are polluted by waste materials. They grow out of control and upset the delicate balance of life in the ecosystem they are in. Some algae produce a bad-tasting oil and contaminate water supplies, or they produce poisons that kill fish or people that eat sea creatures contaminated by their poisons.

Other algae are helpful. In some parts of the world people eat seaweed or feed seaweed to livestock. Substances from a brown seaweed called kelp are used to make ice cream and rubber tires. Scientists are experimenting with growing algae for food. The single-celled alga *Chlorella* grows very quickly in tanks of water when exposed to sunlight. This alga contains a lot of protein and vitamins as

Chlorella *algae can be grown quickly in a laboratory or in large tanks of water. Various kinds of algae may be major food sources in the future.*

well as other food nutrients. In the future *Chlorella* or other algae may become major food sources. Algae and lichens that grow on land keep soil from eroding. When they die, they also provide fertilizer for plants.

MANY SIZES, SHAPES, AND COLORS

Some algae are just a single cell, while others grow in rows of cells and look like threads. Some seaweeds resemble plants. Several algae look like tiny trees at the bottom of the ocean—the sea palm, for example, looks like a tiny palm tree. There are seaweeds that resemble mushrooms, asparagus, or moss. And the light-green sea lettuce looks like leaf lettuce. Kelp looks like a giant brown plant and can grow up to 200 feet (61 meters) long.

Although all algae contain green-colored chlorophyll, most are not green-colored. Algae in freshwater and on land are usually green, but the algae in the ocean are usually yellow-brown, brown, or red. These algae also contain other pigments (colored substances) that block out the green coloring of chlorophyll. Scientists group algae by their color.

Some biologists treat algae as simple nonflowering plants; others consider them protists. All algae have at least one nucleus in their cells. Chlorophyll and other pigments are found in special organelles. Most algae can reproduce by dividing into one or more parts, with each part growing into a new alga. A number of algae produce spores—these special cells are like seeds that grow into new algae. Other algae produce special reproductive cells. When two of these cells join together, they form a new cell that develops into a new alga.

WATER GREENS

Green algae (phylum Chlorophyta) are the algae most similar to plants. They have pigments that are close to those found in plants. They have plantlike cell walls made of cellulose and pectin, and starch is the main storage product, as it is in plants. Because of these similarities, most scientists believe that plants evolved from green algae.

Although some are found in the oceans, most green algae are found in freshwater. Most are microscopic single-celled creatures, but some such as *Volvox* live in colonies, and some form filaments or sheets made up of many cells. For example, *Ulva lactuca*, often called sea lettuce, is a sheet of cells, two cells thick. (However, these multicellular algae do not have specialized tissues and organs as plants do.)

Sea lettuce(Ulva lactuca*) in a shore pool*

Large numbers of microscopic algae can make an entire lake look green. Other types of green algae are big and grow along seashores. Most green algae have flagella during some part of their life cycles.

PROTIST GIANTS

Phylum Phaeophyta, the **brown algae**, contains the largest and most complex algae, found mostly in ocean waters. All brown algae are multicellular. Brown algae contain some pigments that are similar to those of other algae, but others that are unique. They also form different storage products and have components in their cell wall that are not found in other algae. Brown algae are used as fertilizer, as a source of iodine, and as an important source of food in East Asian countries.

Some kinds of brown algae, called kelps, form leaflike blades on a long stalk that is fastened to the sea bottom by rootlike anchors called **holdfasts**. Gas-filled bladders that float at the surface keep the tops of the kelps in the sunlit surface waters. Kelps form large underwater forests. There they are the primary food producer and provide shelter for a whole ecosystem of invertebrates, fishes, and mammals (such as sea otters).

ALGAE IN ARMOR

Taxonomists place **dinoflagellates** in the phylum Dinoflagellata. *Dinos* comes from the Greek for "whirling" and "terrible." Dinoflagellates have both plant and animal charac-

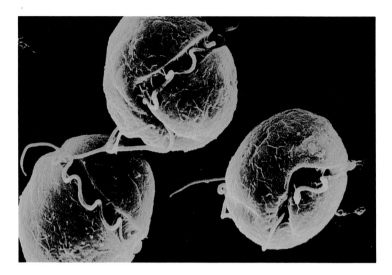

This photo of dinoflagellates clearly shows the groove containing a thin flagellum.

teristics. These small single-celled algae contain chlorophyll. Some get energy from the sun, others eat animals, and some are parasites. Most live in seas, but some live in freshwater. They have a rigid armorlike covering of cellulose plates that makes them look like dented boxes with the corners and edges bashed in. A thin flagellum lies in a groove around the middle of the dinoflagellate like a belt. Another flagellum trails behind.

Together with diatoms, dinoflagellates are major components of **plankton**, the mass of minute water creatures that floats in the surface waters of the oceans. Dinoflagellates are second only to diatoms (a form of golden-brown algae) as primary producers of organic materials in the oceans. They feed on small water animals.

If you're ever out on the ocean at night and see tiny flashes of light in the water like fireflies, it is probably from dinoflagellates. When a ship passes through the water, billions of tiny dinoflagellates light up with an eerie glow. Most dinoflagellates are colored. Red-colored dinoflagellates make the Red Sea red. *Noctiluca scintillans* are as thick as a penny. Sometimes they appear in large numbers, making the water look reddish by day and the ocean glow at night.

When dinoflagellates of the species *Gonyaulax catanella* multiply in great numbers, they cause what is called a red tide. During such a population explosion, a single

A POET'S VIEW

—•—•—•—•—•—•—•—•—•—•—•—•—•—•—

About, about, in reel and rout,
The witchfires danced at night.

That was how Samuel Taylor Coleridge described luminescent dinoflagellates in his famous poem "The Rime of the Ancient Mariner."

quart of seawater may contain five million dinoflagellates. These tiny algae cause a lot of trouble. They produce a waste product that is highly poisonous and kills thousands of fish. (Just a few drops of this poison could kill five million mice!) The *Gonyaulax* toxin can also harm humans. Some sea creatures, such as mussels, store this poison without being harmed themselves. But a person who eats a mussel that was taken from water where *Gonyaulax* was growing can die.

SEA JEWELS

Many taxonomists classify **diatoms** in the phylum Chrysophyta (the golden-brown algae). These tiny algae are often the primary food producers in marine ecosystems. Some of their pigments and storage products are similar to those of the brown algae, but others are unique.

Diatoms have a sort of skeleton. Their hard, glasslike cell walls contain silica, which makes them look like tiny jewels. When diatoms die, the silica "skeleton" settles on the ocean floor and forms a white material called diatomite. People use this substance in pool filtering systems, in insulating and sound-proofing, and as polishing material.

Diatoms come in many different shapes, but all are symmetrical, either bilaterally (one half looks just like the other half) or radially

It is easy to see why single-celled diatoms are called jewels of the sea. The 10,000 species of diatoms form an important part of plankton at the base of the marine food chain.

(arranged in a circular pattern). Some species have cell walls made of a top that overlaps the bottom similar to the way a petri dish fits together. Scientists classify diatoms based on the unique patterns of the cell walls.

Yellow-green algae (phylum Xanthophyta) are related to diatoms, but contain types of chlorophyll not found in brown algae.

FOOD FROM THE SEA

Red algae, the members of phylum Rhodophyta (*rhodo* means "red"), contain the green pigment chlorophyll, plus pigments similar to those found in cyanobacteria. Some red algae have blue pigments in addition to red and green ones. Most red algae are multicellular and have feathery bodies made of interwoven filaments. They contain unique storage products, such as floridean starch, in their cell walls. Red algae often grow with corals in subtropical seas, although some grow in freshwater. They deposit calcium carbonate in and around their cell walls and are important in helping to build coral reefs.

Red algae provide a number of useful products. Nori is a red alga that is part of a traditional Japanese diet. It is dried out and sold in paper-thin sheets. In Japan, China, and Korea red algae are eaten as a vegetable. Agar is a gelatin-like substance that scientists use to grow bacteria in petri dishes. It comes from some types of red algae. Carrageenan, which is also a product of red algae, is used in puddings, laxatives, ice creams, and toothpastes.

PROTIST "PLANTIMALS"

Taxonomists are still fighting over the 800 species of **euglenoids**—protists in the phylum Euglenophyta. Most of these single-celled organisms have plastids called chloroplasts, containing pigments similar to those of green algae, and they carry on photosynthesis in sunlight. Therefore, many biologists classify them among the algae. However, euglenoids do not have cell walls, and they are equipped with one or two flagella. A euglena uses a flagellum to propel itself through the water, or to anchor itself.

Some euglenoids are naturally colorless and feed on organic materials floating in the water. When a green euglena is kept in the dark, it loses its green color and begins to feed like an animal. Placed in the light, it uses photosynthesis to make its own food again. Sometimes when green euglenoids divide by binary fission, all of the chloroplasts go to only one of the daughter cells. The other is unable to photosynthesize and lives an animal-like life. For these reasons, many biologists claim these species as members of the protozoan phylum Zoomastigophora.

Freshwater euglenoids are shaped like partly deflated footballs. (The common pond species *Euglena gracilis* is shaped like a cylinder; another freshwater species, *Euglena spirogyra*, has a large flattened body.) They change their shapes constantly as they swim along. These euglenoids have one or two flagella: one is large and whiplike, but the other is so short that it doesn't even stick outside the cell. Most euglenoids are found in ponds and puddles. Scientists use them as an indicator of pollution—if there are many present, the water is probably polluted.

These small protists are thus a kind of mirror for the whole world of life. All living organisms, from the simplest monerans up to the most complex plants and animals, are dependent on the environment provided by the earth and interact with one another in many complex ways. And human activities can have profound and often unexpected effects on our living world.

IDENTIKEY

Naturalists may use identification keys to help them in identifying various organisms. For example, suppose you scooped up a jarful of water from the edge of a small pond and were examining it under a dissection microscope. The magnifying lenses would open up a fascinating world of strange creatures to your gaze. Here's an "identikey" that would help you to sort them out.

1. Body no fixed shape; moves by extending pseudopods — **Ameba**

Oval body with cilia — **Go to step 2**

Oval or round body with one or more flagella — **Go to step 3**

Elongated, with a crown of cilia — **Go to step 4**

2. Slipper-shaped, with short cilia over entire surface — *Paramecium*

Egg-shaped, with two rows of cilia-like belts around it, snout at front; may be eating paramecia — *Didinium*

Bean-shaped, with a narrow crest of cilia in front and a few large cilia in rear — *Euplotes*

3. Contains organelles with green pigment — **Euglenoid**

Small round body on a long stalk; delicate collar around base of flagellum — **Choanoflagellate**

4. Trumpet-shaped body with cilia around mouth — *Stentor*

Bell-shaped body with cilia around mouth, long stalk — *Vorticella*

Elongated, with a distinct head, trunk, and tapering foot with "toes"; crown of cilia on head looks like whirling wheels — **Rotifer (multicellular, not a protist)**

A LITTLE LATIN HELPS

Knowing some basic Latin and Greek "building blocks" can help you guess the meaning of scientific terms.

a-	without	-fer	carrying
amphi-	both	-form(es)	in the form of, resembling
anti-	against		
archae-	old	-gen	producer
arthr(o)-	joint(ed)	hepta-	seven
auto-	self	hetero-	different
-bacter	bacterium	hexa-	six
bi-	two	homo-	same
bio-	life	kary(o)-, cary-	nucleus
chlor-	green	micro-	tiny
cyano-	blue	mon(o)-	one
-cyt(o)-	cell	-morph	form
deca-	ten	myc(o)-	fungus
dent-	tooth	myx(o)-	mucus, slime
di-	two	nona-	nine
dodeca-	twelve	oct(a)-	eight
endo-	inside	-oid	like
epi-	upon, outer, besides	oo-	egg
		para-	beside
eu-	true	penta-	five
exo-	outside	-phag(o)	eating

-phil	loving	tetra-	four
-phor(e)	carrier	thermo-	heat
phyt(o)-	plant	tri-	three
pro-	before	-troph	pertaining to nutrition
prot(o)-	first		
rhiz(o)-	root	uni-	one
rhod-	red	vir-	poison
sacchar(o)-	sugar	xanth-	yellow
sapro-	dead or decaying matter	-zo(o)-	animal

GLOSSARY

actinomycetes — gram-negative bacteria that form branches of filaments.

adenoviruses — a family of medium-sized viruses that cause respiratory infections, sore throats, conjunctivitis, and intestinal infections.

alga (plural **algae**) — plantlike organisms, mostly water-living; most are single-celled or colonial; all make their own food by photosynthesis.

ameba — a protozoan with a jellylike body that can readily change shape.

antibiotic — a substance produced by microorganisms that kills other microorganisms or stops them from growing.

antiseptic — a substance applied to a cut or other wound to kill bacteria and prevent infection.

Archaea — a domain (category larger than a kingdom) proposed to contain archaebacteria.

archaebacteria — bacteria that live under extreme conditions, produce their own food, are very different from other bacteria, and are believed to be like the first forms of life on earth.

autotroph — an organism that can make its own food by using energy from the sun or from nonorganic materials.

bacillus (plural **bacilli**) — rod-shaped bacteria including free-living forms, symbionts, and disease bacteria (e.g., plague, cholera, and food poisoning).

bacteria (singular **bacterium**) — organisms consisting of a single, relatively simple cell, without a membrane-covered nucleus.

bacterial spore — a tough-walled resting form permitting bacteria to survive in unfavorable conditions.

bacteriophage — a virus that infects bacteria.

binary fission — a form of asexual reproduction consisting of the splitting of a cell into two daughter cells.

biogenesis — the theory that life can arise only from living things.

brown algae — algae containing pigments in addition to chlorophyll that give them a brown color.

capsule — a slimy, protective outer layer found on some bacteria.

cell — the smallest functioning unit of life.

cell membrane — a thin, flexible covering surrounding a cell.

cell wall — a tough, rigid outer covering surrounding a cell.

chlamydia — tiny parasitic microbes causing diseases such as eye infections, sexually transmitted disease, and pneumonia.

cilia (singular **cilium**) — eyelashlike organelles used to produce movement.

ciliates — a group of protozoa that use cilia to move.

classification — the process of dividing objects into related groups.

coccus (plural **cocci**) — a round bacterium.

colonies — groups of cells that remain together but are not specialized for different functions as in multicellular organisms.

conjugation — a kind of sexual reproduction in which two individual cells exchange hereditary material through a tube temporarily connecting them.

cyanobacteria — bacteria containing a blue-green pigment, which produce their own food by photosynthesis; formerly called blue-green algae.

cytoplasm — the cell contents surrounding the nucleus (or the nuclear body in bacteria).

diatoms — single-celled algae covered with intricate glasslike shells.

dinoflagellates — flagellated algae with an armorlike covering of cellulose plates.

disinfectant — a substance that kills bacteria on objects such as dishes or clothes.

division — in taxonomy, a major category in classification; applied to plants, bacteria, and sometimes to algae and fungi; corresponds to phylum in the animal kingdom.

DNA — deoxyribonucleic acid: the chemical basis of hereditary traits.

endosymbiosis — a partnership between two unrelated species in which one organism lives inside the body of the other, to the benefit of one or both.

envelope — the complex outer covering that encloses some viruses.

eubacteria — the "true bacteria" (as opposed to the archaebacteria).

Eucarya — a domain (category larger than a kingdom) proposed to contain all the eukaryotes (protists, fungi, plants, and animals).

euglenoids — a group of flagellate protozoa that may have both animal- and plantlike characteristics.

eukaryote — an organism whose cell or cells contain a nucleus surrounded by a membrane.

flagellates — a group of protozoa that use flagella to move.

flagellum (plural **flagella**) — a whiplike organelle used for movement.

foraminiferans — protists that secrete a chalklike shell through which thin, spinelike pseudopods stick out.

genus — a group of rather closely related organisms.

gliding bacteria — bacteria that move by gliding along on a trail of slime; they produce spores in fruiting bodies.

gram-negative — staining pink to red with the Gram staining system.

gram-positive — staining blue or purple with the Gram staining system.

green algae — plantlike algae that use the pigment chlorophyll for photosynthesis.

herpesviruses — a family of medium to large enveloped viruses that cause cold sores, genital herpes, chicken pox, and mononucleosis.

heterotroph — an organism that cannot make its own food and must obtain organic nutrients by feeding on living organisms (or their products) or dead matter.

holdfasts — rootlike anchors that attach kelp to the ocean floor.

kelp — a brown alga; the largest of the algae.

kingdom — the largest group in the classification of living organisms.

methanogen — an archaebacterium that produces methane gas.

microbe — a microorganism, one too small to see without a microscope. Term usually used for bacteria and viruses.

moneran — a member of kingdom **Monera**; single-celled organisms without an organized nucleus.

multicellular — made up of many cells, usually specialized for various functions.

mutation — a hereditary change in structure and/or function.

mycoplasma — a type of unicellular microbe smaller and simpler than a bacterium; it has no cell wall.

nitrogen bases — building blocks of DNA and RNA. The sequence of the four kinds (A, C, G, and T in DNA) spells out the hereditary instructions in a code that can be translated into proteins.

nucleus — the control center of the cell, containing its hereditary instructions and surrounded by a membrane separating it from the rest of the cell contents.

organelle — a structure inside a cell that performs the same kinds of functions that the organs of animals and plants do.

orthomyxoviruses — a family of medium-sized, spiked viruses that cause influenza.

papoviruses — a family of small viruses that case warts, brain diseases, and genital cancers.

paramyxoviruses — a family of large viruses that cause diseases such as mumps, measles, and distemper.

phylum — a major category in the classification of living organisms.

picornaviruses — a family of small viruses that cause polio, the common cold, and inflammation of the brain.

plankton — the tiny water creatures (both animal- and plantlike) that float in the surface waters of the oceans.

plastid — an organelle in cells of plants and algae, containing chlorophyll (a chloroplast) or stored food.

poxviruses — a family of large oval-shaped viruses that cause diseases such as smallpox and cowpox (but not chicken pox).

prokaryote — a single-celled organism lacking a nucleus surrounded by a membrane.

protist — a member of kingdom **Protista**, including mainly single-celled organisms; a protist has an organized nucleus.

prototroph — an organism that makes its own food, getting energy from the sun or from nonorganic materials.

protozoan — an animal-like single-celled organism.

pseudopod — an extension from the body of an ameba, used to move or to capture prey.

radiolarians — protists with an ameba-like body surrounded by a glasslike skeleton, through which needlelike pseudopods stick out.

red algae — algae containing pigments in addition to chlorophyll that give them a red color.

replicate — to make copies, e.g., of an organism's DNA.

retroviruses — a family of viruses that cause cancers and AIDS.

rickettsia — tiny parasitic microbes causing diseases such as Rocky mountain spotted fever and typhus.

RNA — ribonucleic acid: a chemical carrying hereditary information. (Most organisms have both DNA and RNA, but viruses generally have only one or the other.)

Sarcodina — the phylum that includes amebas and their relatives.

species — a group of very closely related organisms, each able to breed with others in the group.

spirillum (plural **spirilla**) — a spiral-shaped bacterium.

spirochete — a spiral bacterium that moves with flagella; spirochetes cause diseases such as syphilis and Lyme disease.

spontaneous generation — an old theory that living organisms could arise spontaneously.

sporozoans — parasitic microbes believed to be related to slime molds and fungi.

strict halophile — an archaebacterium that lives in very salty environments.

symbiosis — a mutual partnership between two unrelated species, to the benefit of one or both (e.g., nodule bacteria in legume roots and algae and fungi that form lichens).

taxonomy — the science of classifying or arranging living things into groups based on the characteristics they share.

thermoacidophile — an archaebacterium that lives in hot, acidic conditions.

togaviruses — a family of medium-sized enveloped viruses, often transmitted by insects, that cause diseases such as yellow fever and rubella.

true bacteria — one of the two main groups of bacteria; includes most monerans.

unicellular — single-celled; consisting of only one cell.

vaccine — a substance produced from weakened or killed microbes, given by mouth or by injection to stimulate the body's defenses against the live germs.

vibrio — a bacterium shaped like a bent rod.

virion — a virus when outside of its host cell.

virus — a not-quite-living organism that carries hereditary information and can reproduce, but only when inside a living organism.

INDEX

actinomycetes, 32
algae, 11, 20, 31, 35, 36, 38, 39, 48–55. *See also specific type of algae.*
   beneficial uses, 49–50, 51, 53, 54
   classification of, 50
   environments, 48
   nourishment of, 49
   as pollutants, 49, 52–53
   reproduction of, 49, 50
   traits of, 48, 50,
amebas 39, 40, 41, 42–45. *See also* foraminiferans; radiolarians.
   effect on humans, 43
   movement of, 42
   nourishment of, 41, 43, 49
   traits of, 41, 42, 43
amino acids, 13, 14
antibiotics, 25, 32
antibodies, 25
Archaea, 26
archaebacteria, 26–27, 29–30
autotrophs, 27

bacilli, 28, 30, 31
bacteria, 11, 16, 18, 19, 34, 36, 37, 38, 45, 54
   beneficial uses of, 23–24
   classification of, 20, 26–29, 30–33
   disease-producing, 23, 25, 29
   environments, 22–23, 29, 30
   history of, 20, 26
   movement of, 22
   nourishment of, 21, 23, 27
   protection against, 25
   reproduction of, 23, 24
   traits of, 20–22, 27
bacterial spore, 22
bacteriophages, 18, 19
binary fission, 23, 41, 54
biogenesis, 13
brown algae, 38, 39, 51, 52, 53, 54

chlamydias, 31
ciliates, 39, 41, 45–46
   movement of, 45
   nourishment of, 45, 46
   traits of, 45–46
classification, 8–11, 16, 17, 20, 26, 28, 29, 31, 34, 36, 40, 41, 43, 53, 54
cocci, 28, 29, 31, 32

conjugation, 23
cyanobacteria, 20, 21, 22, 27, 31, 32, 37, 54. *See also* monerans.

diatoms 34, 39, 52, 53–54
dinoflagellates, 39, 51–53
DNA (deoxyribonucleic acid), 14, 15, 16, 17, 18, 19, 21, 23, 29, 31, 33, 34, 37, 40

endosymbiosis, 38
eubacteria, 26. *See also* true bacteria.
Eucarya, 26
euglenoids, 39, 54–55
eukaryotes, 21, 26, 27, 34, 37, 38–39

flagellates, 39, 41–42
   beneficial types, 42
   disease-producing, 42
   movement of, 41–42
   traits of, 41–42
foraminiferans, 39, 43–45
fungi, 10, 16, 20, 23, 24, 26, 29, 32, 34, 35, 36, 38, 39, 46, 48